# FABRIC

by Abi Zakarian

## SAMUEL FRENCH

samuelfrench.co.uk

Copyright © 2016, updated 2018 by Abi Zakarian,
All Rights Reserved

*FABRIC* is fully protected under the copyright laws of the British Commonwealth, including Canada, the United States of America, and all other countries of the Copyright Union. All rights, including professional and amateur stage productions, recitation, lecturing, public reading, motion picture, radio broadcasting, television and the rights of translation into foreign languages are strictly reserved.

ISBN 978-0-573-13211-7

www.samuelfrench.co.uk
www.samuelfrench.com

Cover design by © Andrew Pothecary

---

### For Amateur Production Enquiries

#### United Kingdom and World excluding North America

plays@samuelfrench.co.uk

020 7255 4302/01

Each title is subject to availability from Samuel French,

depending upon country of performance.

---

CAUTION: Professional and amateur producers are hereby warned that FABRIC is subject to a licensing fee. Publication of this play does not imply availability for performance. Both amateurs and professionals considering a production are strongly advised to apply to the appropriate agent before starting rehearsals, advertising, or booking a theatre. A licensing fee must be paid whether the title is presented for charity or gain and whether or not admission is charged.

The professional rights in this play are controlled by Alan Brodie Representation Ltd, Paddock Suite, The Courtyard, 55 Charterhouse Street, London EC1M 6HA www.alanbrodie.com.

No one shall make any changes in this title for the purpose of production. No part of this book may be reproduced, stored in a retrieval system, or transmitted in any form, by any means, now known or yet to be invented, including mechanical, electronic, photocopying, recording, videotaping, or otherwise, without the prior written permission of the publisher. No one shall upload this title, or part of this title, to any social media websites.

The right of Abi Zakarian to be identified as author of this work has been asserted in accordance with Section 77 of the Copyright, Designs and Patents Act 1988.

# THINKING ABOUT PERFORMING A SHOW?

**There are thousands of plays and musicals available to perform from Samuel French right now, and applying for a licence is easier and more affordable than you might think**

---

From classic plays to brand new musicals, from monologues to epic dramas, there are shows for everyone.

Plays and musicals are protected by copyright law, so if you want to perform them, the first thing you'll need is a licence. This simple process helps support the playwright by ensuring they get paid for their work and means that you'll have the documents you need to stage the show in public.

Not all our shows are available to perform all the time, so it's important to check and apply for a licence before you start rehearsals or commit to doing the show.

## LEARN MORE & FIND THOUSANDS OF SHOWS

Browse our full range of plays and musicals, and find out more about how to license a show

**www.samuelfrench.co.uk/perform**

Talk to the friendly experts in our Licensing team for advice on choosing a show and help with licensing

**plays@samuelfrench.co.uk    020 7387 9373**

# *Acting* Editions
## BORN TO PERFORM

Playscripts designed from the ground up to work the way you do in rehearsal, performance and study

---

*Larger*, clearer text for easier reading

*Wider* margins for notes

*Performance features* such as character and props lists, sound and lighting cues, and more

---

## + CHOOSE A SIZE AND STYLE TO SUIT YOU

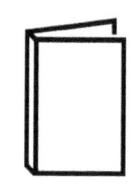

**STANDARD EDITION**
Our regular paperback book at our regular size

**SPIRAL-BOUND EDITION**
The same size as the Standard Edition, but with a sturdy, easy-to-fold, easy-to-hold spiral-bound spine

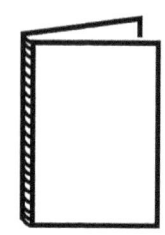

**LARGE EDITION**
A4 size and spiral bound, with larger text and a blank page for notes opposite every page of text – perfect for technical and directing use

---

| LEARN MORE | **samuelfrench.co.uk/actingeditions**

## MUSIC USE NOTE

Licensees are solely responsible for obtaining formal written permission from copyright owners to use copyrighted music in the performance of this play and are strongly cautioned to do so. If no such permission is obtained by the licensee, then the licensee must use only original music that the licensee owns and controls. Licensees are solely responsible and liable for all music clearances and shall indemnify the copyright owners of the play(s) and their licensing agent, Samuel French, against any costs, expenses, losses and liabilities arising from the use of music by licensees. Please contact the appropriate music licensing authority in your territory for the rights to any incidental music.

## USE OF COPYRIGHT MUSIC

A licence issued by Samuel French Ltd to perform this play does not include permission to use the incidental music specified in this copy. Where the place of performance is already licensed by the PERFORMING RIGHT SOCIETY (PRS) a return of the music used must be made to them. If the place of performance is not so licensed then application should be made to the PRS, 2 Pancras Square, London, N1C 4AG (www.mcps-prs-alliance.co.uk).A separate and additional licence from PHONOGRAPHIC PERFORMANCE LTD, 1 Upper James Street, London W1F 9DE (www.ppluk.com) is needed whenever commercial recordings are used.

## IMPORTANT BILLING AND CREDIT REQUIREMENTS

If you have obtained performance rights to this title, please refer to your licensing agreement for important billing and credit requirements.

## ABOUT THE AUTHOR

Abi's plays include: *FABRIC*, produced by TREMers Theatre, played at the Underbelly as part of the Edinburgh Fringe Festival 2016 for which she was awarded a Fringe First Award; *The Best Pies in London*, produced by Rift Theatre for their immersive Shakespeare in Shoreditch festival; *This is not an Exit*, produced by the RSC for The Other Place and transferred to the Royal Court; LULU7, produced by So & So Arts at the Drayton Arms Theatre; *Swifter, Higher, Stronger*, produced by Roundpeg Theatre at the Roundhouse; *A Thousand years*, which was produced by Feast Theatre at Southwark Playhouse. She has also written a short play, *Rip Her To Shreds*, for Undeb Theatre. Abi's most recent play *I Have and I Will Scream* ran at VAULT Festival 2018 and won the festival's People's Choice Award.

Abi is currently developing *FABRIC* for television and working on several new commissions for theatre.

She is represented by Alan Brodie Representation.

## AUTHOR'S NOTE

The rape scene and any other parts of the play related to it must always be portrayed sensitively and with absolutely no recourse to sensationalism, overt brutality or anything that could be construed as placing more emphasis on the visual or physical rather than the words. Topical references to politicians etc can be altered to reflect current times.

FABRIC was first produced by Robin Rayner in association with The Marlowe Theatre. A TREMers production, with the following cast:

## CAST
Leah – Nancy Sullivan

## CREATIVE TEAM
Director – Tom O'Brien
Set and Costume Designer – Alyson Cummins
Sound Designer – Max Pappenheim
Lighting Designer – Zia Bergin-Holly
Movement Director – Lee Crowley
Associate Sound Designer – Daniel Balfour

Producer – Robin Rayner
Associate Producer – The Marlowe Theatre
Company Stage Manager – Amy Clarke
Technical Stage Manager – Gareth Weaver
Production Manager – Suzy Somerville
Press Manager – Laura Horton

FABRIC was revived in 2018

Produced by Damsel Productions at Soho Theatre, London from 11th-22nd September 2018.

### CAST

Leah – Nancy Sullivan

### CREATIVE TEAM

Director – Hannah Hauer-King
Designer – Anna Reid
Lighting Designer – Jess Bernberg
Sound Designer – Anna Clock
Production Manager – Sarah Peters
Stage Manager – Katie Bachtler
Producers – Kitty Wordsworth and Matt Maltby

The production was staged in support of Solace Women's Aid, and followed by a tour of community spaces in London.

# CAST

## NANCY SULLIVAN – LEAH

Theatre Credits: Margery in *The Country Wife* (Southwark Playhouse); Eliza in *My Fair Lady* (Naples Opera House, Teatro San Carlo); Lucy Lockit in *The Beggar's Opera* (Storyhouse); Delores in *Gutted* (Marlowe Theatre); Leah in *FABRIC* (Underbelly Edinburgh) a one woman play for which she won two awards The Fringe First & The Stage Edinburgh Award 2016; LV in *The Rise & Fall Of Little Voice* (Birmingham REP & West Yorkshire Playhouse); Sherbet in *The Fastest Clock In The Universe* (Old Red Lion); Niece in *The Good Person Of Sichuan* (Colchester Mercury Theatre); U/S & played Leah and Sandra in *Beautiful Thing* (West End); Eponine in *Les Miserables* (West End); Anthea in *Judy The Righteous* (Trafalgar Studios); Chloe in *Never Forget* original cast (UK No. 1 Tour), Dorothy in RSC's *Wizard of Oz* (West Yorkshire Playhouse); Jenny in *The Likes of Us* (Andrew Lloyd Webber's Sydmonton Festival).
Film & TV Credits: *Call The Midwife* (BBC); *Afterlife* (Ricky Gervais' new Netflix Series), Sally in *Harry Price Ghost Hunter* ITV and *Les Miserables* movie (Dir Tom Hooper). Nancy is also cofounder and runs W1WORKSHOPS making acting accessible and affordable for all, www.w1workshops.com.

# CREATIVE TEAM

## HANNAH HAUER-KING – DIRECTOR

Hannah Hauer-King is artistic director and co-founder of all-female theatre company Damsel Productions. Hannah started her London directing career acting as Resident AD at Soho Theatre in 2014. She now works as a freelance theatre director alongside Damsel Productions, and a theatre, comedy and cabaret programmer for Fane Productions.
Recent directing work includes: *The Swell* (Hightide Festival); *Breathe* (Bunker Theatre); *Witt 'n Camp* (Edinburgh Fringe); *Grotty* (Bunker Theatre); *Revolt She Said Revolt Again* (RCSSD); *Fury* (Soho Theatre); *Lilith* (Bunker Theatre); *Brute* (Soho Theatre); *Clay* (Pleasance Theatre); *Dry Land* (Jermyn Street Theatre); *Hypernormal* (Vaults Festival). Associate/Assistant work: *Romeo & Juliet* (Shakespeare's Globe), *Radiant Vermin* (Soho Theatre) and *Daytona* (Theatre Royal Haymarket).

## ANNA REID - DESIGNER

Anna Reid is a theatre designer based in London and a graduate with distinction from Wimbledon College of Art. She is the Associate Designer for Damsel Productions.

For Damsel: *Grotty* (Bunker Theatre); *Fury Brute* (Soho Theatre); *Dry Land* (Jermyn Street Theatre). Design credits include: *Schism* (Park Theatre); *Rasheeda Speaking* (Trafalgar Studios); *Collective Rage, Dear Brutus, The Cardinal, School Play* (Southwark Playhouse); *Dust* (Soho Theatre); *Tiny Dynamite* (Old Red Lion); *Rattle Snake* (Live Theatre Newcastle); *I'm Gonna Pray For You So Hard* (Finborough Theatre); *The Kitchen Sink*, *Jumpers for Goalposts* (The Oldham Coliseum); *For Those Who Cry When They Hear The Foxes Scream* (Tristan Bates Theatre); *Dottir* (The Courtyard); *Bruises* (The Tabard); *Arthur's World* (The Bush Theatre); *Hippolytos* (Victoria and Albert Museum); *Hamlet* (The Riverside Studios).

## JESS BERNBERG - LIGHTING DESIGNER

Jess Bernberg is a graduate of Guildhall School of Music and Drama and the 2018 Laboratory Associate Lighting Designer at Nuffield Southampton Theatres. She received the Association of Lighting Designer's Francis Reid Award in 2017.

Designs include: *Drip Feed* (Soho Theatre); *Homos, or Everyone in America* (Finborough Theatre); *SongLines* (HighTide); *A New and Better You, Buggy Baby* (The Yard); *The Marbleous Route Home* (Young Vic); *Reactor* (Arts Ed); *Dungeness, Love and Information* (Nuffield Southampton Theatres); *Devil with the Blue Dress, FCUK'D* (Off West End Award nomination) (The Bunker); *Split, WAYWARD* (Vaults); *Ajax* (The Space); *The Blue Hour of Natalie Barney, The Dowager's Oyster, Youkali: The Pursuit of Happiness, The Selfish Giant* (Arcola Theatre); *The Death of Ivan Ilyich* (Merton Arts Space); *And the Rest of Me Floats* (Birmingham Rep); *And Here I Am* (UK Tour. Co-Design with Andy Purves); *The Poetry We Make* (Vaults Festival/RADA/Rosemary Branch/Old Red Lion); *This is Matty, and He is Fucked* (Winemaker's Club); *Flux: Shadowlines* (King's Place); *SQUIRM* (King's Head/Theatre503/Bread & Roses Theatre/C Venues); *Glitter & Tears* (Bread & Roses Theatre/theSpace UK); *Balm in Gilead, The Same Deep Water As Me, August* (Guildhall).

As Assistant Lighting Designer: *A Streetcar Named Desire* (Nuffield Southampton Theatres); *A Tale of Two Cities* (Regent's Park Open Air Theatre); *A Fox on the Fairway* (Queen's Theatre Hornchurch).

## ANNA CLOCK - SOUND AND MUSIC

Anna Clock is a sound designer and composer based in London via Dublin, working across theatre, film and installation. In her work she aims to create engaging live experiences that challenge audience/performer roles, encourage curiosity and imagination and inspire audiences to listen to their world in new ways. She studied Music and English at Trinity College Dublin and MA Advanced Theatre Practice at Royal Central School of Speech & Drama.
Website: www.annaclock.com.

Recent projects include *Songlines* (DugOut/ HighTide); *Finding Fassbender* (Lydia Larsson dir. Blythe Stewart); *Forgotten Women* podcast series (Peer Productions); *This is a Blizzard* (Flock Ensemble dir. Ana Brothers); *Spun* by Rabiah Hussain dir. Richard Speir (Arcola Theatre); *REACTOR* by Brad Birch dir. Hannah Bannister (Artsed); *The Moor* by Catherine Lucie dir. Blythe Stewart (Old Red Lion); *The Show* by Rowland Hill (Slade School of Fine Art)*;[BLANK]* by Alice Birch for NT Connections (Orange Tree Theatre & Lyric Hammersmith); *CONSTELLATIONS* (Vault Festival 2018); *For The Fallen* dir. John Young (Ballakerneen Studio Isle of Man); *Sonic Fluidities* (UC San Diego, March 2018); *Devil in the Blue Dress* (The Bunker); *Maria* (Omnibus Theatre); *Hilda & Virginia* by Maureen Duffy (Jermyn Street); *Me & My Whale* (Royal Exchange Theatre Manchester, Live Art Bistro Leeds); *Continuity* (Finborough Theatre); *Water Bodies* (LADA, Whitstable Biennale). She was resident artist at Harrow Libraries in association with SPINE Festival 2018.

## MATT MALTBY - PRODUCER

Matt Maltby is the co-founder of Pint-Sized, "two of the most exciting producers of new writing I've met in the last ten years" (Simon Stephens). Pint-Sized have supported three thousand writers over four years, and are resident at Bunker Theatre, where Matt also works as New Work Co-Ordinator. Other work includes Earlsfield Stories for Tara Arts, and producing for artists including Roy Alexander Weise, Eve Leigh, Rachel Bagshawe, and Chris York.

## KITTY WORDSWORTH - PRODUCER

Kitty Wordsworth is Executive Producer and co-founder of Damsel Productions. For Damsel: *Grotty* (Bunker Theatre); *Damsel Develops* (Bunker Theatre); *Fury* (Soho Theatre); *Pint-Sized Goes Damsel* (Bunker Theatre); *Brute* (Soho Theatre); *Dry Land* (Jermyn Street Theatre); *TABS* (workshop, Tristan Bates Theatre). Other producer credits include: *Uncensored* (Theatre Royal Haymarket); *The Naivety, Dick Whit, The Snow Queen, Peter Panto* (Tabernacle); *Siblings* (Live @ Zédel) and *Juliet Cowan: Eat, Pray, Call the Police* (Live @ Zédel). Film producer credits include: *Once Upon a Time's Up* (dr. Denna Cartamkhoob); *Little Hard* (dr. Bel Powley and Alice Felgate); *The Last Birthday* (dr. Jaclyn Bethany); *Sunday* (dr. Daisy Stenham).

## DAMSEL PRODUCTIONS

Hannah Hauer-King and Kitty Wordsworth co-founded Damsel Productions in 2015 to place women's voices centre stage. Damsel Productions hope to be one cog in a larger and crucial movement addressing both the misrepresentation and under-representation of women in theatre. The idea is simple: to bring together women directors, producers, designers and all other creatives to breathe life into scripts exclusively written by women. Damsel Productions aim to provoke, inspire and entertain with true and honest representations of the female experience. Critically successful productions include the UK première of Ruby Rae Spiegel's *Dry Land* at Jermyn Street Theatre, Izzy Tennyson's *Brute* at Soho Theatre and a co-production with Soho Theatre of Phoebe Eclair-Powell's *Fury*. Damsel most recently produced London's first ever all women directing festival Damsel Develops, and Izzy Tennyson's *Grotty*, both at the Bunker Theatre, where Damsel Productions is a resident company.

*With heartfelt thanks to Tom O'Brien and Nancy Sullivan
for the journey we took to make* Fabric.
*Their collaboration on this play is woven into every line.*

## CHARACTERS

LEAH – woman, 34

## SETTING

A room in a house/flat, now.

# ACT I

### Scene One

*A woman (*LEAH*) dances on stage to:*

*"ONE FINE DAY" – by THE CHIFFONS*.*

LEAH   I'm revolting.

*Pause.*

I'm revolting. According to his mum. According to everyone.

*Pause.*

And disgusting.

*Pause.*

I mean, we all know that thing about the mother-in-law. The jokes. Take my mother-in-law, please. No, please.

Look, it started out alright: a Sunday lunch and politeness. Didn't help that his dad was dead – although I don't think they were what you'd ever call close when he was alive. But she took it as she was the only woman he needed; saw me as a threat. Classic really, two women one man. He said, just ignore it Leah. She's only being herself. This just after she's sort of insinuated I'm only interested in him because of his salary. He's like: why would she say something like that? As if I'd make it up. But that's how it goes. Any woman understands this; the enemy is her, me. Him, the field we go to battle on.

---

* A licence to produce FABRIC does not include a performance licence for ONE FINE DAY by THE CHIFFONS. For further information, please see Music Use Note on page v.

*Pause.*

I wouldn't mind but I tried so hard. I know I look a state now but, honestly, when I do my hair, make-up, a nice dress, well, I can look really nice. I scrub up well.

*She grabs a bunch of hair.*

This is all mine you know. No extensions or anything.

*Pause.*

I was blonde when we first met.

*Pause.*

Natural. But I decided to go brunette. Fancied a change. After the blonde…the blonde isn't really me; isn't…doesn't reflect my personality so much.

One of the first things she said to me – just after we'd arrived and we're stood in the hallway, me in my best Orla Kiely dress, her already weighing me up: oh how pretty she is Ben. Taking me by the upper arms; her fingers pressing in just a touch too tight: Well, aren't you a very pretty girl…you must tell me where you get your hair coloured…it looks so real.

*Pause.*

Ben smiling at the two of us because we're obviously besties now. She likes my hair. She approves of my looks. He thinks it's job done. But I knew, deep down I knew. And she did too – that this was all the set up for the long game… I stood there, smiling, smiling; wanting so much to be the perfect girl to bring home, the future daughter-in-law every mother dreams of. I smiled so hard my teeth hurt. Love me, they beamed. You must love me, because Ben does and if he does that should be enough for you. And she smiled right back at me, red thumb prints on my arms slowly fading into pale smudges. But we did the dance anyway; for him. Always for Ben, to keep that smile on his face. That smile we both loved and would do anything to keep turned towards us.

Over the roast chicken she ladled eight potatoes onto his plate, I got three. No questions. A slice of breast for me, four and a leg for Ben. Peas didn't seem to count. I may look small but I love my food. I told her that and Ben laughed, placed his big hand over mine and squeezed it and I think he thought it was all going to be alright then. For a moment. I think he thought it was all marvellous and lovely and his mum and me would become best friends and meet for coffees in town, swap recipes, chat about that new telly series. All those things must have gone through his head as she dribbled the gravy over his food.

*Pause.*

Still. I held out hope because no-one wants to give up at the first hurdle. This was just a Sunday lunch; a get-to-know-you thing. So I explained myself, my background, my life. She offered me a napkin.

*Pause.*

Because I'd spilt red wine on my Orla dress. I use my hands a lot when telling a story, always waving them about like a windmill my mum says. It was only a tiny drop, nothing even got on that thick white tablecloth. Just on my dress, the right-hand boob. Looked awful it did; red on cream. I knew then it was never going to come out; that the dress was ruined.

As she went off to look for a Stain Devil I'd already mentally thrown it away.

When she got back, head shaking sadly – sorry, she didn't have anything for it – but handed me a fresh napkin, I wanted to get up and go to the bathroom, to inspect the damage, try and do something to cover it up; I don't know what, how do you cover up a stain on your right boob? But I didn't move. Just sat there, pushing peas around my plate and listening to Ben and his mum talk about holidays in Sicily and Aunt Irene's hysterectomy; letting my food go cold even though I was starving. Longing for one of my mum's lasagnes. It was too dangerous to risk another stain, another blemish, on this, my first meeting with The Mother. I needed a drink so badly, the wine glass still half full in front of me but no. No, no, no. I smiled at the stories, dropped in a suitable comment here and there: "I've never been skiing, no. But Ben's promised to take me", and, "What beautiful cutlery".

Beautiful cutlery.

"Ben tells me you're a shop assistant".

Very smooth.

Ben's straight in there: "No, no, no, not a shop assistant. Remember what I told you last week? About the promotion?"

I smiled some more, not sure whether to speak.

"Really? But I thought that was how you met...when she served you –"

I met him when he came in to buy a suit. I worked in Savile Row; a high-end place. Well, Ben, he wanted a proper suit and one of his friends'd recommended us as the best place for a bespoke. I was just front of house back then – strictly meet and greet – but I'd been waiting to hear if I'd got a position I'd applied for a few months earlier. I'd been shop floor for two years, came there after working in Selfridges. Always wanted to work in fashion. So when this opportunity for sales manager came up I jumped; filled in the forms, spoke to my boss, even wrote to the creative director. Made it clear I was the right woman for the job. Not a huge increase in salary but I'd be the one to help a customer choose his cloth; which style of suit, all of it.

Some travel overseas with the master cutter on his visits to Europe, if I was lucky. A real step up, and I grabbed it with both hands. And when Ben walked in that day I'd just heard I'd got it; literally ten minutes before my manager Richard had given me the good news. I was so happy, I must've been beaming. So in he comes and we saw each other: he smiles and heads over to where I was standing by the old display cabinet that doubles for a cash desk...only for small purchases; ties, off-the-peg shirts and that – the big sales, bespoke orders, you take the customer to a little room in the back with leather Chesterfields and a tiny cocktail cabinet full of posh booze, and that's where you write – *by hand* – their order out. It's all about making the customer feel valued.

*Pause.*

It's amazing what a glass of whiskey can do to make someone feel special.

*Pause.*

Ben, I'll always remember this, he came straight over to me and said "I need help". "I need help" – how cute is that? I was so happy anyway because of getting the sales manager job, so this was just like getting a cherry on top of a cake – I mean, a six-foot-two, blonde hair, blue-eyed man standing in front of me, asking *me* for help. He was so charming.

*Pause.*

Lots of people say that don't they? "He was so charming" ...well he was, he didn't know what he was doing or what he needed. A suit, he said. I had to laugh at that. Not rude. Not in his face laughing. No, like a little laugh because it was so sweet. Been buying off-the-peg Reiss all his life hadn't he?

I shouldn't have, but the shop was busy and all the sales managers were dealing with other clients so I took him through the basics: cut, cloth, cost. Soon established he had a bit of money to spend but would appreciate a more conservative style; something that would see him through the big three as we call it: weddings, christenings, funerals. He mentioned something about a Bond film – a suit Daniel Craig'd worn as he fell through the roof of a moving train. I knew exactly which one he was on about; we often get requests for Bond suits. So I took him round the shop and we looked at suits together; showed him the Bunches...

They're these lovely big books, full of small squares of cloth; like a folder really but very classy – leather bound, and new ones done every season with all the fabrics we offer. I love the Bunches; love the feel of the covers, the weight of them. They even smell expensive. And I know every single one of those fabrics by heart. Your worsted wools, your tweeds, your super wools... I can tell a yarn twist just by running my fingers over the fabric.

I showed him the Italian navies because navy goes well with blonde hair – adds a certain gravitas – and when I held the book out our hands brushed and I saw there was no ring on his finger. Which is when Richard came over and introduced himself, shaking Ben's hand and shooing me away to tidy the dress socks. And the next thing I know, Ben's being led into the ante room…but at the last minute he turns and winks at me!

How about that? He winked. But not a laddish wink, not an alright darling, no, it was sweet. I thought. It was a letting-me-in-on-a-secret wink.

*Pause.*

He was gorgeous. I knew Richard was giving him the full works but still, I didn't expect him to be gone over an hour in that room. It got close to six; I hung around as long as I could, tidying shelves, fussing over the window display but still he didn't come out. I knew I'd have to leave otherwise I'd miss the six forty-three train. I didn't know what I was hoping for, it was only a wink after all. But just after I'd stepped out of the shop and was no more than ten paces down the road I heard him. Heard him before I saw him. Hey! Hey! He was calling out and as I turned he was right behind me, hand outstretched, so I took it. Yeah, like an idiot. I shook his hand. I don't know why; but how stupid is that? He looked more surprised than anything and we stood there for like ten seconds, hanging onto each others' hands in the middle of the pavement like we were in a rom-com or something – until we both burst out laughing and then he asked me straight out if we could meet for a drink some time.

*Pause.*

First date. Drinks in town. He's the sales director for a big medical company. Prefers cricket to football. Favourite food is steak, rare. Loves skiing and wants to try a sky dive one day. Bought his flat dirt cheap a few years ago and now it's worth a ton more. Only child. Very close to his mum. Hates those massive eyebrows on women.

Likes Jason Statham films and would never vote Tory but can understand why some people do. When he goes to the toilet I google on my phone to find out why some people do vote Tory. Walks me to the station where we have a kiss and he presses into me as I stumble back against the wall, my bag banging into his groin so he mock staggers away claiming I'm killing him with my hotness.

Second date. Dinner at an amazing seafood place, where he pays. Tells me I look like a blonde Emma Stone. Makes me try oysters which I hate because I read somewhere they're still alive when you do that shucking thing but I don't tell him this and instead swallow, smile and go mmmm. We agree to go skiing together even though I've never been and the idea terrifies me a bit but he talks about a place called Verbier and the name makes me think of fancy candles. We take a taxi together to my place but he doesn't even try to come in. We kiss for three pounds worth on the meter and his hand rests on my thigh, gently, his fingers just touching the edge of my dress.

Third date. Meet him in town after work for drinks with a couple of his friends. We sit in a posh bar and drink gin martinis, which I've never had before; they're so strong but I sip them slowly, not wanting to seem uncool. His friends, Luke and Phil, join us and are really lovely to me; ribbing Ben about how he'd managed to pull such a hottie. He keeps his arm over my shoulder the whole time and I like how he's so protective of me. Afterwards, he puts me in a taxi and I see him hand the driver a couple of twenties. He kisses me through the open window, promises to ring.

Fourth date. He comes over to mine for dinner. I say mine, at the time I was sharing a flat with Kate, my best friend. Every boyfriend I've ever had since I was fifteen, Kate'd be there, giving them the once-over, making sure she approved. Kate's always been the vivacious type – men all over her whenever we went out. She's really glamorous. And some of the fellas she's been out with…city types with so much money…little pictures, swiping left, swiping right.

Still, I could tell she was impressed with Ben; with the bottle of wine he'd brought. She stayed long enough for a glass, firing questions: you'd better not muck my best mate around or you'll have me to answer to, that kind of thing. She's laughing though and he's laughing and I remember her saying the same thing to Mark Reynolds when we were in sixth form.

She got off with him two days after he'd finished with me 'cause I wouldn't give him a blow job.

*Pause.*

But she left, eventually. Heels clicking down the hall as she pulled on her jacket. Don't do anything I wouldn't do! Ben raising his eyebrows; either in hope or disapproval, that big smile following her as she left. Then we ate and, after finishing the wine, he kissed me as we sat on the sofa, the subtle pressure of his legs against mine, the heat and hardness enveloping me. He whispered that he wanted to make love to me, that he couldn't wait any longer.

*Longer pause, she fans out her hair.*

Afterwards he told me I was definitely potential wife material. Four dates and I'm potential wife material!

*Pause.*

I was so happy.

*Pause.*

The happy girl for weeks and months.

*Pause.*

My mum loved him. How could she not? When they met he brought flowers, patiently explained what his job entails. By the time we were eating the trifle everyone was smitten, as I knew they would be. Mum, my sister Deenie, even Nan, and she's not easily pleased. But as I've come to realise...

*She pauses, slips into contained anger and pain.*

...but as I've come to realise, no-one is good enough for a son but anyone is good enough for a daughter.

*Pause.*

Him. Mum beaming as he handed over the flowers; flashing me a wink and then squeezing his arm and giggling like a teenager as she showed him through to the front room, seating herself opposite him on the sofa, perched on the edge of the chair and straightening her shoulders. Deenie jokingly asking about brothers even though she's married to Useless Mark and got two kids. But he answered all the questions with that big smile of his, having second helpings of everything and wishing I'd inherited Mum's cooking skills. Her and Deenie laughing and eyeing him up like the prize he was; not believing I'd bagged a bloke like him – but he picked me, he picked me that day he came in for his suit. Me.

*Pause.*

It was Deenie who got the old photos out, budging him up on the sofa, folding out the albums on his lap. Mum leaning over behind him, giving dates, locations, bits of embarrassing information. Nan sat opposite and stared at Ben the whole time – like she was waiting for something to happen. He did well considering she's not one for small talk – kneeling to greet her; taking her tiny hands in his. As he pulled himself upright again I saw her snag a quick touch of jacket fabric, quietly asking: "One of yours?" I shook my head and she let her hand drop, sighing that she was parched with all this excitement, sending Mum flapping off into the kitchen for the best teacups.

*Pause.*

It's funny. I thought I'd be more relaxed bringing Ben home, but it was strange. I felt like I did when we went to his mum's: a bit uncomfortable, a bit awkward. I don't know why. He was so relaxed; those blue eyes casting over everything, tracing my life in that photo album, in my nan's face, the Crown Derby plates on the wall. By the time we left, said goodbyes in the cramped hallway, Mum flinging her arms around him and telling him he was gorgeous; her delighted smile when she turned to me: "Don't mess this one up Leah".

*She stifles a scream.*

*Pause.*

Eight months. Eight months, one week and two days.

*Beat.*

I was thirty. And the sense of having just made it; having just closed the deal, was everywhere. Most of all from my mum, whose relief was almost too much to bear, but I shoved it aside and went into her happy embrace. Her little girl, getting married! At last! She kept saying. At last!

*Pause.*

I would move into his flat after the wedding. Kate decided to move back in with her parents because they had a massive four bedroom house and she was sick of all her money going on rent anyway. She told me I was so lucky; Ben being so fit and having his own place plus the Audi. She said I was the luckiest bitch alive. Naturally, she was my chief bridesmaid.

*Pause.*

And then we all lost our minds.

*Pause.*

I had a rock this big…

*Pause.*

Nan was pretty much the only one who stayed sane. She'd sit in her chair and listen and nod as every inch of air was taken up with wedding talk. Mum took to ignoring her, saying she was a killjoy because her wedding was a knee-length duchess satin then sandwiches and stout down their local.

Mum said Nan was bitter. But I sat with her one day; not long before the wedding – I was pretty much exhausted with making lists – and I brought us some tea, thankful Mum and Deenie were out. It was chilly: are you cold Nan, should I turn the heating up? Come here: I just moved to her and took her hands. They…they felt like towels dried on the radiator, her grip so tight, pushing the stone on my engagement ring into the side of my finger where it hurt but I didn't want to say anything so let her keep holding on.

"It's not too late Leah. Beer and skittles and fifty-two years". Beer and skittles. I didn't know what she was going on about but she wasn't finished…"A dress shouldn't cost near on two thousand pounds. Shouldn't weigh more than a newborn'. Don't be daft, I said, this is my one chance to be a princess, the one day it's all about me. Don't let your tea go cold Nan. I thought she was done but she was rummaging around in her cardigan pocket; she fishes something out and thrusts it at me…a photo; only six by four if that, and creased and battered round the edges.

I looked down: a knackered old black and white photo of her and Grandad and about eight family and friends.

*Pause.*

It was her wedding day. Nan's face... I thought I was looking in a mirror I looked so much like her. And she's stood next to Grandad, their fingers almost touching but the creases down the middle of the picture make it hard to tell; years of folding and unfolding worn a gully between their hands but their faces turned so slightly towards each other I see it. I see that they're in love. Despite the years gone by, I see it.

*Pause.*

The two of them.

*Pause.*

I don't know how long I sat there looking at the photograph.

*Pause, very present in the now.*

I know what love is.

*Longer pause.*

I made sure the wedding plans didn't affect my work even though they cut me lots of slack when I needed to go to all the appointments. I made up the hours because I didn't want them to think I wasn't reliable, especially as I'd just started in my new position, but they were brilliant; they even gave me a beautiful bespoke wedding garter made from my favourite fabric; a nine-ounce worsted tiny check in black and cream. It was trimmed in a cream lace and had mine and Ben's names embroidered on it. I loved it.

*Sound effects: Voicemail message "You have one new message..." etc, then:*

**LEAH'S BOSS** *(voicemail)* Leah. Richard Stokes. Been trying to reach you for a few days...well, in light of...um...we felt it would perhaps –

*Coughs.*

– better you take extended leave. We...the best way forward. Um...do call me...do call if you need to... OK. Thank you.

*The message ends.*

**LEAH**  I always wanted to go to New York. I thought it would be like a movie: me and Ben strolling through Central Park, walking down Fifth Avenue with coffees in our hands, stopping in front of Tiffany's and taking pictures of ourselves gazing at all the jewellery. At night we would go to bars only locals go to and eat hotdogs from steel carts on street corners.

And we could visit Far Rockaway.

*Saying it to herself, it's a beautiful place for her.*

Far Rockaway.

It's a place, right at the end of one of the subway lines. Saw a picture of it in a book; got a bit obsessed with it.

Sounds like something in a fairy tale doesn't it? I so wanted to go...

*Beat.*

Ben thought this was hilarious.

*Pause.*

We went to the Maldives for our honeymoon. A place flattened by sunshine. Looking out to sea every morning from our private villa I saw what looked like the results of a perfect experiment on the colour blue. Lying there staring up at what I thought was the sky but might as well've been a giant blue alien watching me; wondering when I would divide, multiply and then, inevitably, die.

*Sound effects: Voicemail message "You have one new message..." etc, then:*

**LEAH'S MUM**  *(voicemail) (nb. this is to sound almost on the point of hysteria – possibly unintelligible by the end)* Leah, sweetheart! We're already here! Where are you? It is a *gorgeous* shop; we're picking out dresses already! Hurry up otherwise your sister will've drunk all the champagne.

*She laughs.*

Yeah, they've given us shampoo! How posh is that? God, it's lovely here; you're going to love it. Hurry up sweetheart will you.

*The message ends.*

LEAH  There I'm stood. Stood there. On a little white satin covered box in the middle of the room, about a foot high. And you get led to it. Led, like I can't find my own way there. And there's my mum sobbing already, and Deenie's got her hand up to her mouth, eyes wide. Everybody: "Oooh".

Like a goddess. Resplendent. Up I go, hitching the dress to make my ascent. And it's so heavy. I wasn't quite prepared; even though I'd got it on, had walked in it. Until it was in my arms I didn't know just how much of it there really was. You've got to feel the weight of it to know, you know?

And I'm stitched up in the back. There's boning.

There's corsetry. There's buttons. Oh, there's so many buttons.

I looked like a present that's been gift wrapped by a bored sales girl.

There I am. I stand there. On my tiny satin box. Waiting to be opened. Back then, I reckon, I look delicious.

*Pause.*

Or ridiculous.

*She shifts.*

Sexy. I wanted to be sexy. Sexy but classy. Yes. It all starts off a bit fifty shades but quickly turns to shit.

You can't give that crap away can you? You never see that many copies of Middlemarch or Frankenstein in the charity shops do you?

*Pause.*

I read a lot now. Like, really read. I love Frankenstein. Mary Shelley wrote that when she was nineteen. Nineteen! Can you believe it? Nineteen. Married to a poet and travelling round Europe; one crazy holiday in Switzerland and: bam! think I'll write a book...

*Laughs.*

I mean, what had I managed by nineteen?

*Pause.*

And everyone thinks the creature is Frankenstein. That poor old patchwork man. I thought that too, until I read it. And then you realise, it's the man who made him; he's Frankenstein, he's the real monster...

*Pause.*

But now...now it's all this...this fan-fic shit. I can't believe I bought into it. And Ben did too; although you realise too late that his version of sexy and your version of sexy are several hundred downloads apart. Watching a porno together; starts off fun, some wine, the dimmers way down. He chooses the film because you wouldn't know where to start and before you know it there's fucking all over.

He's loving it, just seeing the fucking, hearing the noises, knowing the plot, but you get fixated on the faces, the determination in their eyes; skin so tight you worry it'll split like sausages you haven't pricked before frying. The jerking bodies bent into position after position. This is not like daddy's stash of Razzles with its coy ladies opening themselves up across the staples, confusing your ten-year-old self with their abundant hair. No, this is something you want to turn off but Ben is intent, so you try to get into it but the forensic detail shrinks your desire into a tight ball in your stomach, and the relief you feel after the violent climaxes end is huge.

*Pause, she gathers herself.*

The women pinned down, the words angry, violent, cruel. Packaged up as bondage and safe words like it's one of them glossy M&S ads. Like it's something you buy.

*She pauses, thinks.*

*Pause, whispering.*

I am terrified of my wedding dress.

It...it can stand up on its own it's so wide. Empty, but...traces of my skin stuck on the insides. Bits caught on the boning, the sequins, the net. If anyone wanted to clone me then all they'd need to do is just scrape a bit of me off one of those tiny satin-covered buttons that run down the spine of the dress – there's a hundred of them, take your pick. Like DNA, a bridal helix. Clone an army of brides from a single satin-covered button.

*Pause.*

There was a stain on it.

*Pause.*

Oh it's gone now; dry cleaners saw to that. No need for soda water, because the stain came after the wedding: after the food, after the red wine, after the cake. I navigated that assault course perfectly; not a drop of anything got on me; this dress stayed pristine. I don't think I even sweated into it. No, the stain came later.

*Pause.*

*Reflective.*

It's so beautiful though. Monstrous. But beautiful...

That's the trouble. The stain.

*Pause.*

Our bridal suite was fancy. A four poster, two fat sofas facing each other across a low glass table spread with glossy mags, port in a decanter, heavy curtains with massive tassled ties.

*Pause.*

He said –

*Pause.*

Because it was a special occasion.

*Pause.*

The most perfect day.

*Pause.*

Come on. It's our wedding night.

*Pause.*

My wife.

*Pause.*

Come on. For me. Do it for me.

*Pause.*

Our wedding night.

*Pause.*

How could I refuse?

*Pause.*

I was his princess.

*Pause.*

He said.

*Pause.*

Running a finger up the inside of my arm. His lips on my ear. His other hand into the masses of white, rustling in there, reaching down between my legs, not getting purchase, withdrawing, reaching again, the lace and net stuffing up his route as all the while he traced a line on the inside of my arm: come on baby, come on darling. For me. For me. I giggle, don't be daft Ben. Come on.

He pushes his mouth over mine and we do the Hollywood kiss. I rustle like tinder; wait, wait I say, let me get out of thi –

But no, he's turned on by all this fluff and I'm struggling to unhook all the buttons but, baby, baby, leave it on and I've got no choice because it's like flypaper this thing I'm in. I don't really want to; did it once before and I didn't like it but he wanted to and there's so much of this material. He burrows inside me pushing the skirting over my back, you're in here somewhere he pants and I so want to be the delightful sugared almond taken in his arms, taken up to bed to do the husband and wife thing even though we've been doing that for over a year but somehow the rings on our fingers make it all proper again. And all the while he's getting exasperated by the massiveness of my dress; where the fuck are you he wants to know. I try to help, to turn, to spread my legs but he's adamant he wants it this way and in the confusion he covers my head with tulle so suddenly I'm underwater in a world of cream, hang on Ben I'm muffling, hang on let me I just but it's no good because he's found me, my Victoria's Secrets knickers pulled down without the due respect they deserve, because right then and there, in our bridal suite, I am a cupcake pushed over the back of one of the massive sofas and he eases himself between my legs and I want so much to please him, to be the perfect wife. It's not that hard is it? I think to myself and the cock is his cock after all, my husband's cock and I love it as much as all of him because it's a part of him so I let it happen and the creamy fabric all around me shudders and billows and I listen as he tells me he loves me and the other stuff he says, the stuff I don't really want to hear on my wedding night, gets swallowed up by the netting, caught like fish.

When I hear him spit on his hand I think of the good sex we've always had, the strong, wet, messy sex but it still doesn't quite stop the stab of pain I get as he puts his cock in. I'm concentrating, thinking of the great sex I'm having, the carefree woman I am because Ben loves me and I'm his wife and it's my wedding night and it's beautiful honestly, it's the best and I'm making the noises although I can't be sure he can hear me but I make them still because that's how the story goes, on our wedding night and he's right, it's a special occasion.

*Pause.*

When he's done he collapses on top of my back, his face buried in the cloudy fabric as I bend like a wishbone over the back of the sofa. Eventually he moves. The rustling I hear. The words of love I hear. The pain reassures me, despite the slow mess I feel sliding down my inner thigh; something I mistake for love sliding down my inner thigh coming to rest on the garter top. He loves me. He loves me full stop.

*Slightly longer pause.*

Then he wipes his cock on my beautiful dress and walks away.

*Long pause.*

Later on, lying in bed, I said my new name out loud, but quietly so as not to wake him. Mrs. Cavendish. Leah Cavendish. Mrs Leah Cavendish. I said it over and over again, trying to get to sleep.

Then it hit me. I could've hid in the bathroom. I could've locked the door, pretending to prep myself. He might've had a think and decided against anal on our wedding night; might've realised... But what good would that do? What would that say? Me locking myself in the loo to get away from my husband on our wedding night? The love of my life.

*Pause.*

*Sound effects: Voicemail message "You have one new message..." etc, then:*

**DEENIE** *(voicemail)* Hey Leah! It's your little sis here. Remember me? Ha. You're, like, impossible to get hold of. Anyways, got some news so give us a bell when you can. Bet you can guess though –

*Tiny pause.*

– so call. Loves ya.

*The message ends.*

**LEAH** I love him. And he loves me. I know what love is. And it's not a three-foot wide dress or a silver Audi. I know what love is: it's fat curries every Friday night and slow Sundays on the sofa. Day to day it was all I wanted. And I love him. Like it's a dirty word nowadays; a bit lame, a bit bad TV. But I do.

*Pause.*

Not long after we got back from our honeymoon Ben said "Let's look for a bigger place". Why? "This is too small, plus it's my place and we need somewhere which is for both of us". I told him I was happy here, I loved his flat. But he kept on, he rubbed cream into my sunburnt shoulders and kissed my neck and told me we could afford it; that we should be buying somewhere bigger at our age, that we needed a house because a house was a home.

*Pause.*

So every night after work we'd look at the houses he'd found: period semis with gardens and garages; insisting on three bedrooms. After two weeks we found a place to view.

*Pause.*

His mother arranged the solicitors; paid for them too. Anything for my son she said when I called to thank her for her generosity. I sent flowers the next day and promised she'd be the first guest after we'd moved in, which only took a couple of months because the flat sold really quickly to a cash buyer. An investor, Ben said.

*Pause.*

*Sound effects: Voicemail message "You have one new message..." etc, then:*

BEN'S MOTHER *(voicemail)* Leah, dear. It's Rachel. I can't get hold of Ben. I know you must be absolutely swamped with everything for the housewarming so I'll bring my apple tarte tatin. I know you struggle with sweet things and it is Ben's favourite. See you tomorrow.

*The message ends.*

LEAH Nan stayed home; she couldn't get out as much any more and was getting over a nasty bout of flu but Mum was there, and Deenie and Mark came with the kids. It was the first time we'd all been together since the wedding, Rachel in a bouclé suit like she's Jackie bloody Kennedy, smoothing the cushions after the kids dive-bombed the sofa, her face a tight smile. We gave them the tour and then sat down for lunch. Deenie drank too much, baby in the crook of her arm, Mark sat there mute, as usual, only coming alive when Ben turned on the huge flat screen TV. I brought in the coffee: Is that a little bump I see?

My mum.

Ignoring her I handed out the coffees but she asked again, this time adding something about my ankles, the amount I'd eaten at lunch. There's this weird silence and I looked up to everyone watching me; Ben frowning slightly. Are you saying I'm getting fat? No, I'm saying you *should* be getting fat...and she adds – just in case I don't get the massive subtlety – with *babies*.

*Pause.*

Those conversations that quickly go from "do you want kids" before you're married, to "when are you having kids" after. The friends of friends telling you it was the best thing they've ever done, the nurse explaining why your smear test hurts on account of a tight cervix – "never given birth you see", the younger sister who warns you about your age, your decaying eggs...

*Pause.*

So I laughed, said something about there being no hurry. Ben gave me a look. Later on, after everyone had gone, he said look at your sister, she's two years younger but she's got three kids. I carried on loading the dishwasher. I felt like I'd failed an exam or something.

*Longer pause, to herself.*

I never understood what all the rush was.

*A long pause, then suddenly galvanised.*

Kate's a great organiser. She called me one day and was like for fuck's sake, are we dead yet? Can you all please just ditch your husbands and your kids and come and get absolutely rat-arsed like we used to before you all turned into such boring old farts? I was the first one to sign up; but in the end there was six of us – all in our thirties, but not done yet.

When I told Ben I might crash at Kate's he was cool, said he might get a few of the boys together, but I knew he wouldn't, he was just saying it to make it seem equal or something. But I didn't care, I just wanted a night off from being Mrs Cavendish. I got out my red dress, the one Ben first kissed me in, the one I knew I looked good in. Silk, fitted but not tight tight, and stopping just above the knee.

"Hey hey hot pepper sauce!" said Kate when she saw me, and Ben stood in the hallway, fists deep in his pockets, watching as I pulled on my jacket. You going to kiss your wife goodbye? said Kate, hopping from foot to foot in impossible heels, nostrils flared from the same kind of crappy coke we used to snort together as twenty-year-olds off our kitchen table. Ben knew to peck me on the cheek so as not to mess up my lipstick. Have fun, he said. Have fun, don't do anything I wouldn't do. We won't, we won't, Kate's jabbering, pushing me out the door towards the waiting taxi. I look back over my shoulder to Ben as he shuts the door, his face already turned away.

*Sound effects: Voicemail message "You have one new message..." etc, then:*

**WITNESS CARE OFFICER** *(voicemail)* Hello Leah, Bryony here. Hope you're feeling a little better today. I've got the court dates now so could you call as soon as possible and we can go over a few things. Call me any time. Thanks. Bye.

*The message ends.*

**LEAH** The drinks are green. A green so transparent I remember staring into it and seeing right through the liquid, through to the bottom of the glass and down onto my bare knees wondering how they got it so clear. I want to fall into it, it's so inviting but someone jostles my arm and I come back into the thudding now; a girl murdering a song on stage.

Drink!

I down the shot. It burns so bad but I slam the glass down on the table and we all cheer; let out that "whoaaaa!" you do when you're throwing drink down your throat like your gut's on fire. Another round comes, I reach for a glass; it's a different colour this time; a soft pink, it smells like strawberries and cream. We drink again and roar our approval; I feel a hand on my shoulder; a big hand, a man's hand, and it's freezing, like they've just come in from the cold and I turn, half expecting to see Ben, my lips parted in a smile, sweetness as I lick them. But it's not Ben. It's Phil; Ben's old school mate, one of our ushers. I've not seen him since the wedding over a year ago but Baby, he calls me. His big hand resting on my bare shoulder, the cold in his fingers making me prickle and I can only gaze up at him.

Baby! Leah! Fancy seeing you here! I am thrown, like I always have been, by his absolute confidence. Oh, a works do, he tells me, boring as fuck… Ben not here?

All our friends are shifting round now, and Kate's eyeing him up. She turns around on the sofa and kneels to greet him, her arms and his around each other as they kiss cheeks. I suddenly feel –

**DJ** *(sound effects. Offstage)* Leah! Leah Cavendish!

**LEAH** Which means it's my turn on karaoke. I get up, pulling my dress down at the thigh and up at the bust; it's both rising and falling, stupid thing. Those two shots on top of the prosecco and a gin and tonic power me towards the stage, and the lights are twirling, and the douf-douf-douf of filler music stuffs up my ears. I reach for the mic held out by the girl who sang before me, her version of Let It Go having provoked wild applause despite her singing Have A Go whilst twerking. Here you go babes she said, handing me the microphone which was slick with her sweat. I saw lipstick on the top of it, lipstick in the tiny holes. How many different lipsticks were on it? The forensics of it, the shots in my stomach, all of the thudding around me as I stepped on stage and stood in the lights, my hand up to my eyes, tasting strawberries and still feeling the cold of those thick fingers.

*Music starts.*

But the music starts and in that instant I forget. I forget the lipstick-stained mic. I forget the cold. I forget the fact I've drunk so much my heels don't pinch anymore. Because now I sing my song. I sing it. I don't need the lyrics on the screen; I know them off by heart and the room is alive and the volume goes up and up and the lights are in my eyes and my heart beats loudly and my head fills with the song and it's so loud and my heart beats and I can feel it I can feel it feel it feel it.

*Starting to sing, with great joy.*

"NEEDLE IN A HAYSTACK" by THE VELVELETTES**

*As the song ends* LEAH *returns back into now, panting with adrenaline.*

*Pause.*

People are clapping and cheering.

I'm suddenly really thirsty. I hear the DJ saying things about me, about my singing but it all has that weird, distant feel like when you're under water and I just want to get off stage and get some water, hoping Kate's got some nurofen. I turn to leave the stage and trip over the microphone cable. I struggle to get up, the next girl to sing already standing there with her hand out to take the microphone and everyone's laughing at me and I look down at myself, at my dress, and I see these horrible stains on my stomach, weird splotches that make it look like I've been stabbed because it's a red dress and the stains, the drink or whatever that I've spilled over myself makes the fabric go darker. I start to think I *have* been stabbed, and I'm trying to get up, heels slipping, skidding on the floor, I'm holding my stomach. I hear the other song and the girl singing, singing and I'm crying I think, a bit, and my knees, whatever, it's awful I just want –

*Pause.*

Then he's there.

Those big, flat hands pick me up, warm now and under my arms lifting me from the floor. Thank God for Phil I'm thinking. Thank God for Phil.

Baby girl, what a state you've got yourself into. Come on.

And he picks me up and carries me away.

---

**** A licence to produce FABRIC does not include a performance licence for NEEDLE IN A HAYSTACK by THE VELVELETTES For further information, please see Music Use Note on page v.

*Long pause.*

I don't think I'd had that much to drink. I remember everything from that night. Tiny details. Tiny things. I remember. I remember... I do.

*Pause.*

Kate...

*Pause.*

Everyone drank that night. He had –

*Pause.*

*To herself, muttering.*

No matter how many times I say it.

*Long pause.*

He carried me to the smaller bar round the corner; you can see it on the film. There's like these little booths with tables in them, it's a bit quieter there. I drank some water and he had a look at my ankle.

I had to put it up on his lap; we were sat opposite each other and the table was between us so I had to put my foot on his lap you see. I said, I know I said, I wanted more water but he said no, no, you'll throw up. But I was shaking my head which was aching, like a migraine coming on, saying I want some more water my mouth is so dry. He got me up...then it's...this is the bit where I'm not...it's –

*Pause.*

I was going to the loo. I remember trying to go back to the sofas where the girls were and I had one shoe in my hand. I needed to pee, on the way back to the girls on the sofa but somehow, somehow he...he got me into the disabled toilet. He said the ladies was full and I was...he said I was –

*She stops, intensely distressed, clenched.*

*After some time.*

I bought this dress for our first date; Ben said it was his favourite of mine. He told me I looked indecently beautiful in it. Which I used to think was a compliment. And it's silk, which is why the stains ruined it. There's vomit, urine, blood and semen on this one. And fecal matter too. Which I suppose is not surprising considering I was in a toilet, on the floor. They found all those things despite my having washed it; despite having taken it to three different dry cleaners. Amazing isn't it?

Blood, piss, shit, puke and spunk. All on a tiny red silk dress that I thought I looked so hot in.

*Pause.*

The funniest thing is that this was returned to me.

As if I'd want it back.

*Pause.*

Did they think I might want to wear it again? Might want to dress up nice for a night out?

*She shakes her head.*

All those fingers on it. All those hands. All over it as they passed it to each other. I don't know what they were looking for; what that shitty piece of fabric would offer up about me. Would one of those washed-out piss stains make clear whether I was lying or not? Or the cum? How did that get there if not by me letting it?

*Pause.*

Forensics.

*She waits.*

That and CCTV.

*Pause.*

I take his arm. See. My arms are around his neck when he picked me up. Switch to another camera. The bit when I'm in the booth with him; he brings me a full glass and I sip at it as his hands are underneath the table, manipulating my foot, my ankle. See. At one point I rest my head on the table top and he can be seen moving my hair out of the way. Then he moves around to my side of the booth and he puts his arm under my shoulder and slides me out. Switch to another camera, I am trying to go in one direction he is pulling me in another. I see this.

He was trying to assist me though; I was "confused". I needed the loo. Switch to another camera. We are leaning against the disabled loo door; my back against it, him against me. My hands are on his belt, but the CCTV is very dark here so my hands are pushing his groin away from me. His arms are pinning me to the door. His arms are around me. His arms were pinning me to the door. I have one shoe on, the other is in my hand, but the CCTV is very dark there, because of the angle of it, but my shoe is in my hand and I am pushing his groin away from me.

Forensics found a small, almost imperceptible, puncture mark on his stomach. The shape was similar to that of a stiletto heel end but it was also very similar to that of a shoe stud, like the kind possibly found on a rugby boot.

*Pause, perhaps to herself.*

Disregard.

*Pause.*

One minute and twenty-seven seconds. One minute and twenty-seven seconds. Before the door opens, or before the door is opened.

You cannot see what my other hand, the one without the shoe, is doing at that point because the CCTV is dark and the angle of the camera makes it difficult to say conclusively but the door to the disabled loo becomes open and I fall into it, one of his hands grabbing at me as I fall backwards, the other hand lifting up quickly, as if it had been on the door handle but also as if it had been in his pocket because the camera angle cannot say for sure. The hand that grabs me makes purchase on my silk dress, upper left portion, the seams across the bust showed evidence of stress but not of tearing or coming undone.

My legs skittle apart like Bambi, the stiletto shoe on my left foot bends alarmingly in at a right angle and the other shoe drops to the floor.

But the CCTV is dark and by the time the door closes with us both inside it's as if we were never there.

*Longer pause.*

It stinks. I'm gagging because of the smell but not being sick. He is over me, one hand on the back of my neck the other on my left breast. He tells me I want it, that I'm so ripe for it. He is putting his lips on my neck and I remember, I remember twisting this way and that. It was disgusting. The wet. Down on my knees now he has a handful of my hair as I'm pushing and gagging I remember, his belt buckle, BOSS stamped on the metal. Of course I said no. Of course I said it. It's pointless. I was saying no please please no not this please no I don't want no please and he's saying yeah yes course you do you were all over me come on baby I know you do come on come on easy I'm saying no I remember I'm saying no his hands inside my thighs I'm saying no he says yes yes pulls down my knickers fingers inside me I'm crying it stinks he's over me behind legs skitter the dress up around my waist careful now he said come on baby I know you like it up the arse trying to scream but gagging on the smell as he as he the rim of the toilet hitting my stomach again and again fixing my eyes on a broken tile on the wall watching the crack of it pushing myself into the crack of it the rim of the toilet seat hitting my stomach he's telling me I want it I want it watching the crack feeling the rhythm of his thrusts the pain is the pain is I remember stop I say he's inside me and I scream but no sound comes out and he tells me I am nice and slippy but I don't know how he can think that because it hurts so bad I want to scream yeah you like that baby he's panting over me my stomach on the my knees the shoe I see the other shoe my the door when we fell backwards and into this place he fucks and fucks and I give up.

*She stops.*

*Very long pause.*

Eleven minutes and forty-four seconds. I gave up.

I remember.

I remember.

He was laughing at one point, a massive square hand resting on my back. I heard him laughing whilst I stared at the crack in the tile on the wall.

*Pause.*

After he'd finished he pulled his cock out of my backside and reached for some toilet paper but there wasn't any so he rinsed himself off in the sink. Sweet, he said, doing up his trousers. Sweet.

He lifted me off the floor, pulled up my knickers. He spent some time rearranging me I remember. He smoothed my hair back off my face. Be our little secret, baby Leah yeah?

*Sound effects: Voicemail message "You have one new message..." etc, then:*

**KATE** *(voicemail)* Babes! We looked for you but guessed you must've gone home. God we were pissed. Ha! Fucking awesome night though. Forgot how fit that Phil is. Get Ben to put in a good word for me. Anyways...give us a bell when you get this. Laters.

*The message ends.*

*Long pause.*

I stayed off work for a few days, said I was a bit under the weather. At first Ben was understanding then he told me to go to the doctors but I sat on the sofa looking in the direction of the TV. After three nights of coming home to a dark kitchen he sat down and asked me what was wrong.

I said I was just tired and needed to catch up with myself. We ate takeaways for a week. I locked the bathroom door when I showered and stayed up late watching series after series. He left me to it but there's only so many nights you can fall asleep on the sofa before the husband starts to notice you're not being the wife. So he sits beside me one evening after clearing away the curry cartons. He leans into me, concern twitching in the vein above his eye and it's all I can do to keep the food down, because he has no idea, no clue and if I were to tell him I'm afraid of what he might do. But his hands cover mine – beautiful hands that could close over me and squash it all away – he asks what's wrong, what's the matter, how can he help with whatever it is that's troubling me? And I looked down at the coffee table and see a tiny blob of mango chutney on it and I concentrate hard on it as I hear Ben asking me again, what's wrong baby? What's wrong?

I am in a tunnel and I move away from his voice even quicker than I thought I could. I focus hard on the mango chutney, try to think of a happy time: our wedding day, but that freezes my heart so I scrub it out and look for another time, and I see the day we met, the inside of the shop, the big leather seats but those leather seats they remind me so and eventually I hear a noise so insistent startles me back into the room and Ben is frantic as he grips my arms and says over and over Leah! Leah! Leah!

*Pause.*

I'm sick all over the coffee table. Ben leaping away Jesus Christ Leah what the fuck? And the panic in his voice because he knew then, he knew it wasn't just some shit about feeling under the weather.

*Pause.*

So I told him.

*Sound effects: Voicemail message "You have four new messages..." etc, then:*

*Note: the voicemails can overlap, rising loudly and melding into a mess of voices.*

**LEAH'S MUM**  Leah, sweetheart, you must call me. Please Leah. We're all worried sick about you. Where's Ben? I can't get hold of him. Oh God Leah –

**POLICE WOMAN**  Mrs Cavendish, this is DCI Shawcross, your SOLO. Can you give me a ring at your earliest convenience: I need to go over your statement with you –

**KATE**  Leah, I've got to give a statement to the police. Shit Leah, this is really bad. Can you call me? I need to...look, I can barely remember that nigh –

**BEN**  ...um, Leah. I'm at my mum's. I... I don't know if I'll make it back tonight. I've had a lot to drink so probably shouldn't drive... I... I, er... I'll call you. Just... I'll call you.

*Voicemail ends.*

*Pause.*

It's amazing how quickly everything fell apart. Much quicker than I ever thought it could. Which is funny really, when you consider how slowly the mechanics of justice took just to get me into that little box, raised up, everybody looking...

**LEAH** *stands as if in a court witness box.*

*Listening.*

Yes, I did have alcohol on the...the night in question, yes.

*Listening.*

Um. I had some prosecco –

*Listening.*

I had three.

*Listening.*

Right. I also had about four shots of –

*Listening.*

I think it was four.

*Listening.*

I was quite tipsy. I wanted some wat –

*Listening.*

I do think it made me less steady. I fell on the stage –

*Listening.*

It was foggy, my head.

It was... I could sing, yes, I... but you know how you can be drunk but still –

*Listening.*

Well yes, I do agree.

*Listening.*

No. I did not want to do that.

*Listening.*

No. He...he was the one who...who... I did not kiss him.

*Listening.*

No. He... I was turning away. I did not want his mouth to be... near mine.

*Listening.*

I did not. I did not do that.

*Listening.*

I didn't want him to think I was being...he was Ben's...my husband's friend –

*Listening.*

No. My husband and I are not currently living at the same address.

*Listening.*

No. It is not a lie. I did not make this up.

*Listening.*

No. I did not "conspire" –

*Listening.*

He brought me some water.

*Listening.*

Because I couldn't get away. He...he had a hold of my foot...

*Listening.*

I didn't want to seem rude.

*Listening.*

I was crying because I'd hurt myself on the stage, after the song.

*Listening.*

I wasn't trying to seduce him. I wanted some water, I wanted to go back to my friends.

*Listening, shaking head vehemently.*

No. I did not touch him. I did not –

*Listening.*

I know it looks like that on the film...but I didn't. I didn't...

*Long pause, direct, accusatory.*

No-one believed it of him. Couldn't see it in his face; couldn't believe it of a man like him. Not Phil; good looking, good job Phil. Proper man, him. Not one of those types. Not a monster. All you saw was your sons as he stood in that box and spoke in a low voice, stumbling through the sex we'd had like a teenager; not knowing what he was doing, but knowing it was only wrong in that it was his friend's wife who had thrown herself at him, begged him, pleaded and then demanded to be had. You saw your sons up there and you wanted it over with. Me the dirty liar, hanging out of a slut's dress. Made monstrous by my sex.

*Long pause.*

It's like when people look at photos of serial killers, child murderers and that. You look at the photos and: Oh look, we say, they look like a wrong 'un. They always looked like a wrong 'un. I see it, we all say. I see it.

*Pause.*

So what does that mean they saw when they looked at me? All along, I mean. I must look like I wanted it. I must look like I asked for it. I must look like the liar.

None of them, not even my own mother, sees a reflection anymore.

*Long pause.*

Just a dirty stain.

*Pause.*

Opinions are like one of those giant waves: smashing anything that isn't exactly like it, and what it doesn't destroy it just sweeps up and carries along with it so there's no other choice, no other option but to have the same opinion. #dirtyslutcheater, #upforit, #bogskank.

*Pause.*

And Ben.

*Pause.*

The few things we shared after the trial were silences. Traded in for divorce agreements, signatures on a stack of papers, more ink spent. In the end though I was glad to be done; marriage is a game you start playing from an early age and I am done. That big white dress calls to me still but the language sounds different now…years and years desperately trying to get into it when really it's a caul you're born with. So that three-foot-wide dress I can't leave just yet; maybe one day when I've moved again, but not yet. I need my ghost, my shit-stained ghost but mine still.

*Pause.*

*She stops. Collects herself.*

I wore what Nan used to call a "useful" dress.

*Pause.*

Wore it to her funeral. We buried her three weeks after the trial; me, Mum and Deenie. The church was full but half of the people there gawkers, looking for the tell on the back of my neck. A priest going on about a woman he didn't know, about a life fulfilled; marriage and children achieved instead of just accrued. All those stops along the way of a life, a small wooden box in the ground as we fell apart above it. Not quite dead, but something close.

*Pause.*

I'd not long been moved out but Mum looked like an empty dress, and I wondered how much of this was all my fault, if only I'd swallowed that curry back down and washed my hair and wiped the coffee table clean. If only I'd gone to bed with Ben that night and said "I am Mrs Cavendish" out loud in the darkness.

*Longer pause.*

*She starts to cry, softly then gathers herself again.*

A memory. When I was a little girl, six or seven I think, I sat at the kitchen table as we ate dinner; me, Deenie, Mum and Dad – because he was still there back then. Bored by boiled vegetables and tuning out the hatred going back and forth between my parents I found a hang thread on my tartan pinafore. Whilst I pushed the food around on my plate with a fork in one hand my other fingers worried away at this thread.

It was impossible to stop, and the feeling I got when I felt the thread come away, knew that it was unravelling, it was like some kind of euphoria and I knew that I was going to keep pulling until I couldn't pull anymore, both exhilarated and terrified. I didn't look down once but my fingers kept on and it wasn't until Deenie looked over and screamed, alerting my parents to what I was doing that I froze, and my mother slapped my hand away and somehow it was all my dad's fault. He just stared at the handprint-sized hole spread over my stomach, my pink vest showing through and he shook his head. What are we going to do with you Leah? And I worried then that something would be done.

*She stands and moves to a doorway.*

Revolting.

*Pause.*

I was undone. Every thread unraveled: the stitches meant nothing, the pattern gone. I watch the lines, the colours, patterns, all disappear before my eyes.

*Pause.*

I was that woman once, that woman called Leah. And I knew everything I wanted; put there in pink when I was born, even.

*She has autonomy.*

Once I was sure, like a small girl is always sure, but now…but now the threads are mine. Mine.

*Pause, ready.*

Tomorrow I will wear—.

*She moves away.*

*Blackout.*

## End

# THIS IS NOT THE END

**Visit samuelfrench.co.uk and discover the best theatre bookshop on the internet.**

A vast range of plays
Acting and theatre books
Gifts

samuelfrench.co.uk
samuelfrenchltd
samuel french uk

Milton Keynes UK
Ingram Content Group UK Ltd.
UKHW020721101024
449496UK00011B/266